"We need to be reintrodu
Morefield does this by avo........ ... ...s.o..a. caricatures and instead
giving us animated and active followers of Christ. Followers who, as humans, both struggle and triumph, both fail and follow Christ. Not only is this book helpful and relevant to our lives, it also built my faith as it interacted and applied the Word of God."

> **Doug Ashley**
> Lead Teaching Pastor, Longview Evangelical Presbyterian
> Church
> Longview, TX

"Theology matters. Through the lives of three Reformers, Stephen Morefield not only illustrates this but also applies it to our lives on a practical level."

> **Matt Graham**
> Senior Pastor, Christ Fellowship Church
> Fort Collins, CO

"Don't dismiss this as simply an 'historical book!' In *Living & Active* Stephen Morefield blends engaging history with unique and timely application to our modern Christian lives."

> **Glen Massey**
> Associate Pastor, Southport Presbyterian Church
> Indianapolis, IN

"We've all been bored at one time or another as a history teacher drones on with a breathless procession of dates and names from the past. In *Living & Active*, Stephen Morefield has done more than spare us from this yawn. The lives of Luther, Calvin, and Knox are devotionally recounted as a mirror to show us our own glories and warts, all done in a way to help us behold the beauty of the gospel and the power of God's Word."

> **Benjamin Vrbicek**
> Lead Teaching Pastor, Community Evangelical Free Church;
> Author of *Don't Just Send a Resume* and *Struggle Against Porn*,
> and coauthor of *Enduring Grace*
> Harrisburg, PA

BesorBooks

100% of the profits of this book will be given toward the continuation of the Reformation in Europe, specifically through Serge missionaries in the Czech Republic.

VOL. 1

SCRIPTURE THROUGH THE LIVES OF LUTHER, CALVIN, AND KNOX

—————————— STEPHEN R. MOREFIELD

Stay up to date with Stephen's writing at facebook.com/besorbooks.

Special thanks once again to the Jaeger family for their kind provision of the Wee Scottie Cabin for the writing of the first draft. What a perfect place to behold the majesty of Christ's creation! Thanks to beta readers Doug Ashley, Aaron Denlinger, Matt Graham, Doug Massey, and Benjamin Vrbicek; faithful pastors who lent their time and wisdom to improve this book. Thanks as well to my incredibly talented sister, Ashely Foote, for the exceptional cover design. Finally, thanks to Alexandra Richter for her outstanding editorial work. Every author needs an editor of her caliber.

Cover design: Ashley Foote
Interior design: Stephen Morefield and Benjamin Vrbicek
Author photograph: Doug Storie

Trade paperback ISBN: 978-1-7322755-6-0
Mobipocket ISBN: 978-1-7322755-7-7

To Dave Partin, Bill Carpenter, and Darren Casper:
The faithful men who pastored and mentored me. While
history may not remember your names as it has the subjects of
this book, your ministry is of no less value. Thank you for
loving, serving, and laboring for the local church. You've made
an incredible difference in my life.
– Stephen

LUTHER, CALVIN, AND KNOX TIMELINE

1483   Luther born in Eisleben

1505   Luther becomes a monk

1509   Calvin born in Noyon

1514   Knox born in Haddington

1517   Luther posts Ninety-Five Theses

1521   Luther appears before the Diet of Worms, begins exile at Wartburg Castle, translates New Testament into German

1525   Luther marries, writes *Bondage of the Will*

1533   Calvin is forced to flee France

1536   Calvin publishes *Institutes of the Christian Religion* and receives call to Geneva; Knox becomes a priest

1538   Calvin banished from Geneva

1540   Calvin marries

1541   Calvin returns to Geneva

1546   Luther dies in Eisleben; Knox's mentor, Wishart, is burned at the stake

1547   Knox pastors St. Andrews Castle, becomes a French galley slave

1549   Knox released, preaching in England

1554   Knox exiled, serves in Geneva with Calvin, serves also in Frankfurt

1555   Knox marries and briefly returns to Scotland

1558   Knox writes *The First Blast*

1559   Knox returns to Scotland

1564   Calvin dies in Geneva

1572   Knox dies in Edinburgh

CONTENTS

INTRODUCTION: WHY STUDY THE REFORMATION? 1

CHAPTER 1: LUTHER'S LIGHT 9

CHAPTER 2: LEARNING FROM LUTHER 21

CHAPTER 3: CALVIN'S CALLING 31

CHAPTER 4: LEARNING FROM CALVIN 43

CHAPTER 5: KNOX'S ANCHOR. 53

CHAPTER 6: LEARNING FROM KNOX 63

CONCLUSION: GLORIOUS RUINS 71

ABOUT THE AUTHOR 73

ALSO FROM BESOR BOOKS 75

NOTES 79

WHY STUDY THE REFORMATION?

For most honest individuals, the thought of studying 500–year-old church history sounds about as exciting as watching someone else watch paint drying. We may wonder, what does this have to do with me? What does this have to do with the twenty-first century? Could anything be less relevant? Even for the devout Christian, we wonder whether we have more civilized times to learn from, whether old-fashioned theology debates really could affect our love for Christ and neighbor, and if we can really justify spending precious time on this. These questions are fair, honest, and important to address before expecting any reader to engage in a work of this nature.

As a lover of church history, I'll tip my hat and confess my bias; I'm captivated by church history and have been deeply shaped by it. That being said, I'm confident that each of the above objections simply fall short of reality. Though it's far from an exhaustive list, let me give you five brief reasons to dive into the drama, beauty, horror, wisdom, folly, and living history left behind by the Protestant Reformation.[1]

The Reformation Changed Everything for Everyone

Suppose you have no interest in Christianity. Even if that is the case, understanding the Reformation is crucial for understanding the world you find yourself living in. Modern views of education, government, literacy, individuality, science, sexuality, work, and, of course, religion have profound ties to this great event. One noted scholar put it like this, "The Reformation of the sixteenth century is, next to the introduction of Christianity, the greatest event in history. It marks the end of the Middle Ages and the beginning of modern times. Starting from religion, it gave, directly or indirectly, a mighty impulse to every forward movement, and made Protestantism the chief propelling force in the history of modern civilization."[2] The Reformation truly turned the world upside down and things have never been the same. Understanding this event and its continuing repercussions is crucial for an informed view of not only history but also the present world in which you live.

The Reformation Is Wildly Entertaining

I'm putting myself up for examination here, but history is only boring if it's poorly told. And the Reformation is no exception. This time period is filled not only with an explosion of knowledge but also literal explosions on battlefields. Between theology debates and warfare, there's no shortage of daring escapes, devilish murders, trickery, espionage, and conflict between popes, pastors, queens, peasants, and lords.

Even for those who love more subtle or emotional drama, there's the shocking scandals of runaway nuns proclaiming the goodness of marital intimacy with their new pastor-husbands and societies rejoicing in newfound liberties such as simply eating sausage during the Lenten season! Add to this the nearly apocalyptic outbreaks of the plague, royal household dramas, and bold stands for gospel truth and there's not much that happened during this time period that isn't fascinating. Entertaining as all this is, we also do well to soberly remember that these stories are not fiction. Real eternal lives were won and lost in the Reformation, and this should both heighten our interest and deepen our thoughtful reflection.

The Reformation Challenges the Modern Church

If the modern church will listen, the Reformation has much to teach. On one hand, the Reformation challenges the church to follow Christ boldly. In an age of mega-churches, celebrity pastors, and the so-called "prosperity" gospel, it is clear that something valuable has been lost, at least in the West, when we consider the sacrifices, dangers, and leaps of faith required for common men and women who sought to obey Christ in all things during the Reformation. That the modern church might grasp the gospel with such clarity as Luther; that we might experience worship with the purity of Zurich and Geneva; that we might find the courage of Knox or see Christ in all of Scripture as Calvin; that we might cherish the Scriptures as Tyndale or seek to spread the gospel into all of society as Zwingli; that we might see glory, grace, mission, and worship in our daily duties as the mothers, farmers, bakers, and salesmen of the Reformation. What a challenge the Reformation gives us.

But we also have a warning to heed. The Reformers made many mistakes. They used harsh words towards enemies, trusted in politics and warfare instead of prayer, fell into pride as success came, undervalued unity, and lacked charity towards allies. The Reformation was full of broken men and women. Though God did great things, this was no return to Eden. While ignoring the Reformation is foolish, idealizing it is equally dangerous. Instead, we must take the good and bad and allow the modern church to be both warned and challenged, both encouraged and humbled.

The Reformation Made Much of Christ

Despite all of their imperfections, the Reformers were unified in shining the spotlight on Christ as he is revealed through Scripture. Every Christian desperately needs this focus in their lives. The message of the Reformation, as summarized in the five sayings known as the *Solas,* points us to our greatest needs. Through these sayings our eyes are peeled away from ourselves, our efforts, this world, and its teachings and are instead plastered upon the Savior. We turn to *Scripture alone,* God's Word, as our ultimate source of truth over all human tradition and teaching. Through Scripture we are called to trust in *Christ alone* as the only mediator between mankind and God the Father; Christ is our only representative and advocate, the only one who can work on our behalf. By this, we see that our salvation is by *grace alone.* Nothing we do could possibly forgive our sins or earn us the righteousness that the Father requires. Christ's work provides this grace fully. We receive all of this by *faith alone*, by trusting in the identity, promises, and work of Christ. Finally, all of life is therefore to be lived *for the glory of God alone.* We no longer seek our agenda or even the glory of the Church. All glory, all praise, all honor, all worship is directed to Christ.

Has there ever been a time in history where this was needed more than now? Our particular age is tormented and torn by the competing yet simultaneous siren calls to self-worship and submission to culture. How many Western churches flip the *Solas,* trusting culture instead of Scripture, working for culture's approval rather than Christ's, pushing works that will get us and our congregations labeled as *good* and *reasonable* folks, putting faith in our desires rather than Christ's, and hoping to show that Jesus is loving but certainly never exclusive in his work. Though it always looks different, every age truly shares our need. What we, with all people throughout history, need most is Christ. The Reformation, though imperfect, makes much of Him and points us in a wonderfully different direction than our culture.

Studying Church History Is an Act of Worship

Finally, beyond even the Reformation, the reality of a good and sovereign God reminds us that the study of history, with proper perspective, is the study of the living Savior. From eternity past, to the making of creation, from the guidance of Israel, to the incarnation, from the resurrection to Pentecost, from the Reformation to the twenty first century, we recognize the work of the Savior among his people for the sake of the world. When history, in all its brokenness, blemishes, and blunders, is seen within the grasp of his hands, it becomes an opportunity not only to learn but ultimately to worship. Through the eyes of faith, history gives us ample opportunity to worship the Savior's wisdom, perseverance, patience, and his unstoppable kingdom that advances in the darkest moments and flourishes in unlikely yet stunning ways. To study history, especially church history, is to see how the Savior uses broken vessels for his glory. As we consider the lives of Luther, Calvin, and Knox, our eyes must quickly turn to their Savior, their hope, their God. For this reason, this work seeks to serve as a match—a match that lights something larger, something lasting, something that burns with an undying flame. Not only do I hope you are inspired to read more from these men, but mainly I hope that you'll be drawn to find their Savior more beautiful and more worthy of your worship as you do read. For this reason, each chapter will move us beyond the lives of these men and toward the Word through which they learned to worship the Savior in increasing devotion and dependence.

Finally, let the reader note that two chapters have been devoted to each Reformer. The first uses a passage of Scripture as a window not only into that Reformer's life but also the reader's. The second functions as an appetizer, introducing the reader to the Reformer's own writing with recommendations for further sampling and exploring. Dig in and enjoy!

"For I am not ashamed of the gospel, for it is the power of God for salvation to everyone who believes, to the Jew first and also to the Greek. For in it the righteousness of God is revealed from faith for faith, as it is written, 'The righteous shall live by faith.' "

Romans 1:16–17

LUTHER'S LIGHT

Born into a German, Catholic family in 1483, Martin Luther was a gifted student preparing for a lucrative and respected career in law.[1] This, however, was suddenly and dramatically changed by a violent thunderstorm and a dash of terrified superstition. Although he was academically successful, Luther struggled with crippling anxiety, depression, and a spiritual fear of judgment throughout much of his young life.[2] And so, when he found himself trapped in a thunderous countryside storm, Luther assumed the worst and desperately called out to the only person he thought might care, his family's patron saint: "Help me, St. Anne, and I will become a monk."[3] Luther survived the storm and, true to his word, ditched his legal career and became a monk.

Unfortunately, life in the monastery only increased Luther's anxiety as he was forced to focus upon the source of his troubled state: guilt before a perfect and holy God. In response, Luther did everything a monk could possibly do to find peace, writing, "I wearied myself greatly for almost fifteen years with the daily sacrifice, tortured myself with fastings, vigils, prayers, and other very rigorous works. I earnestly thought to acquire righteousness by my works."[4] When this failed to quiet his soul, Luther turned to wearing out his mentors and superiors by confessing every sin he could have possibly committed, droning on for hours at a time.[5] With his background in law, Luther knew that he stood guilty before the ultimate Judge and he was finding little hope of avoiding the sentence he knew he deserved.[6]

What about you? What do you do with your guilt? While most of us have not gone to such lengths, we all experience guilt. Sometimes it's just a prick of the conscience while at other times something darker and deeper is revealed in our hearts. It happens when your child asks you why you're always glued to your phone. It happens when your spouse catches your eyes wandering. We feel it when we lose our temper, catch ourselves cutting corners at work, or when we reflect on a relationship we've been neglecting. No matter a person's beliefs, everyone deals with guilt. The real question is *how* do we deal with it?

Do you push your anxious guilt down and ignore it, as Luther did until the storm? Do you make rash vows to do better knowing full well that it probably won't work? Do you work hard, beat yourself up, and live for others in the hope that this will make up for any shortcomings? Or are you proud enough to think that you're good with God simply based on the type of person you are? Whether we're in denial or not, we all have a guilt problem.

And this is why, like Luther, we desperately need the Word of God, especially Paul's letter to the Romans. It is in this epistle, specifically Romans 1:17,[7] that we are called to live by faith, or active trust, in what God has done. Luther discovered that he had to trust in something to deal with his guilt. And by learning the hard way, Luther realized that purposeful denial, prayers to the saints, honest confession, and hard work in ministry all failed to get the job done. Instead it would take faith—faith in what Jesus has done, which is made known in the gospel.

How Does the Gospel Work?

How we think the gospel works is essential for our faith. And, surprisingly, the gospel first gives us bad news. It reveals God's standard. Our God, the triune Father, Son, and Holy Spirit as revealed in Scripture, is fully good, perfect, and just all the time and in every way. In short, God is righteous. This is good. An all-powerful God who is just a bit wicked or unjust would not be good news. That being said, it only makes sense that God demands the same of us. A perfect God cannot accept evil or sin in us or the world. To do so would be to perpetuate the very opposite of his character. God's righteousness requires perfection. But this creates a problem and, hence, our bad news. Luther saw this right away when he first read these words in Romans 1:17: "For in [the gospel] the righteousness of God is revealed." As a monk, Luther confessed that he raged against this passage and against God. Luther assumed that God had simply revealed his perfect standard without revealing a means of meeting that perfect standard.[8] If that was true, this wasn't good news; it was a death sentence. Luther knew he couldn't live up to God's righteousness. He couldn't meet the standard. He knew that a gospel like this only brought guilt and condemnation.

As Luther wrestled with his guilt and anger, he watched his church, the Catholic Church, offer him and others an easy way out. Indulgences were for sale, and these could be purchased from the church to secure forgiveness with God. Christians could also buy these waivers of forgiveness to shorten deceased family members' time of suffering in the fictitious spiritual halfway realm known as purgatory. Specifically, Joseph Tetzel had been sent by Pope Leo X to Luther's town to sell these quick fixes. Tetzel was a professional who combined both salesmanship and guilt to sell as many indulgences as possible while famously exclaiming, "as soon as the coin in the coffer rings, the soul from purgatory springs!"[9] While many Christians didn't know any better, Luther's personal wrestling with sin and guilt prevented him from being fooled. Luther knew his church members were being robbed and given a false assurance of forgiveness. A simple coin surely couldn't cover the cost of rebellion and sin against the good and just Creator of the Universe.

In his anger at Tetzel, Luther turned back to wrestle with God's Word, specifically Romans 1. What Luther discovered changed the world. Luther began to understand that the gospel not only reveals God's requirement but also meets it. "At last, by the mercy of God, meditating day and night, I gave heed to the context of words [in Romans 1:17] ... Here I felt that I was altogether born again and had entered paradise itself through open gates."[10] What had Luther discovered in the context of this passage? The key was faith: "For in [the gospel] the righteousness of God is revealed from faith for faith, as it is written, 'The righteous shall live by faith'" (Romans 1:17). The gospel does not call men and women to measure up to God's righteousness by their own works but rather calls them to put their faith and trust in the righteousness that comes from God.[11] In other words, when Jesus the Son died on the cross, he took our sins and gave us his righteousness—God's righteousness—as a gift.[12] This is a "gift from God that renders people acceptable . . . in his sight."[13] Simply put, in the gospel, God gives us what he requires. That's incredible news.

Sadly, most modern, Protestant, and even "Reformed" Christians don't fully appreciate the beauty of this. When Christians are asked what Jesus has done for them, many understand that their sins have been forgiven but very few understand that something else has been given in the place of those sins, the very righteousness of Christ. This is crucial. Without God's righteousness, we might be temporarily forgiven but we wouldn't be forever changed or given anything other than a blank slate that we could only muddy and blemish with our continued brokenness and sin.[14] We'd still be "sinners." While we do continue to struggle with sin, Luther understood that our identity had fundamentally changed from "sinner" to "righteous child of God." God has declared and made it so for us. This is how the gospel works. It changes who we are forever.

What Does the Gospel Do?

Our modern society struggles with the gospel because it fails to understand our need for it. We are told that we are "okay" and we desperately want to believe that we and others are truly fine. Because of this, the gospel's promise to powerfully save us is ignored. But Scripture tells us otherwise, "for all have sinned and fall short of the glory of God."[15] And because we've all fallen short, Romans 1 gives us a blunt verdict: "For the wrath of God is revealed from heaven against all ungodliness and unrighteousness of men, who by their unrighteousness suppress the truth."[16] Simply put, God not only requires righteousness but will also destroy everyone and everything that is not righteous. Do you see what's at stake? Apart from God's righteousness, this life is meaningless, our work is wasted, and the future we face is the just wrath and punishment of God. It's a harsh truth but it's accurate and fair. And there is good news. No one wants to be told by their doctor that they have cancer, but no one complains when the doctor has a guaranteed cure.

Here's the good news: "For I am not ashamed of the gospel, for it is the power of God for salvation to everyone who believes, to the Jew first and also to the Greek" (Romans 1:16). Any type of person can be saved. There's no disclaimer on age, race, sex, income, family background, sin struggle, or past history. Any type of person can be forgiven, receive the righteousness of God, and be transformed. This gospel has gone not only to the people of God throughout history, the Jews, but also to the Greeks, which is shorthand for everyone else.[17] There's no type of person who can't be saved. While Paul says the gospel's power is "boundless," that is, open to all types of people, it is also "boundaried," as Timothy Keller has said.[18] What is the one boundary? The gospel is salvation to "everyone who believes" (Romans 1:16). True belief, or faith, is the one requirement. Only those who have accepted their desperation, and who are not ashamed to rely upon God in such a way, receive this gift.[19] At its core, this means personally trusting Christ and his work.[20]

This idea is far simpler than the church of Luther's day had made it. And when he understood it, Luther wanted to share this news with as many people as possible. After his views became known, Luther was forced to spend years of his life fleeing persecution. But this time was not wasted. As he spent his first months of exile hiding in Wartburg Castle, he did something that was punishable by death. Luther translated the New Testament into German so that the regular people of his nation could actually read the Bible and discover for themselves that there was a remedy for their guilt and sin.[21]

Do we share Luther's excitement about the gospel? It is, after all, "good news." If not, it's likely because we've missed just how powerful and open the gospel truly is. If we aren't convinced of our freedom and the power of the gospel toward any who believe, we'll tend to keep it to ourselves. We become ashamed of it. When we sulk in the guilt of our sins instead of basking and resting in forgiveness, we'll be prone to focus on the guilt of others as well. Feeling judged, we become judges. In a similar manner, if we've been motivated by guilt over sin in the past, we'll be prone to motivate others by guilt as well. Feeling burdened, we pass out burdens. However, if we realize what the gospel has truly done, we'll not only have a balm for our guilt, but we'll be able to stop piling it upon others and instead point to the freedom found in Christ.

When Does the Gospel Make a Difference?

For Luther, the gospel just kept getting better. From beginning to end, it made all the difference concerning his guilt and anxiety. "For in [the gospel] the righteousness of God is revealed from faith for faith . . ." (Romans 1:17). The righteousness that we need from God is revealed from or by faith. By our faith, we can accept God's gift of righteousness. This is the moment that changes everything, that brings us from death to life. But how do we get faith? Does the gospel only make a difference after we choose to have faith? In several places throughout Scripture,[22] the apostle Paul clarifies this by saying that before we have faith we are dead in our sins and utterly helpless. And dead men can't have faith. In

Ephesians 2:8, Paul tells us that faith is the gift of God. In light of this additional context, the picture in Romans 1 becomes clear. God gives spiritually dead men and women the gift of faith to receive his righteousness. It is "from faith" (Romans 1:17). Luther preached that the gospel is not chiefly about what we have done but about what God has done before we ever believed!

And this same gospel keeps us until the end. "For in [the gospel] the righteousness of God is revealed from faith for faith . . ." (Romans 1:17). The gospel not only comes from faith but it also comes for faith. God doesn't just save us by faith and leave us on our own but rather he saves us for a life of faith. What God starts he finishes. This idea ties into the end of this passage, which quotes the Old Testament prophet Habakkuk in saying, "The righteous shall live by faith" (Romans 1:17, Habakkuk 2:4). Once God declares you righteous by faith, he gives you faith to keep trusting him and his work day by day, year by year, for the rest of your life. The gospel makes a difference from start to finish. It gives us life in God and keeps us there.

The gospel didn't make Luther perfect in this life. He continued to struggle with a temper, foul language, anxiety, and being uncharitable to other Christians such as the great Reformer Ulrich Zwingli.[23] Even still, the light of Romans 1 changed him forever as he increasingly found peace and courage in God's promise of faith in the midst of difficult circumstances.

After posting his Ninety-Five Theses, which were statements against the state and teaching of the Catholic Church in light of what he'd discovered about the gospel, Luther was called to trial. Surprisingly, he chose to go despite the clear risks to his life. After stating his beliefs, Luther was ordered to recant and turn back to the beliefs he had embraced as an anxious, terrified, and neurotic monk. Knowing his life hung in the balance, Luther asked for time to pray and reflect. The following day he gave this answer to his accusers and persecutors: "I am bound by the Scriptures I have quoted and my conscience is captive to the Word of God. I cannot and will not recant anything, since it is neither safe nor right to go against conscience. I cannot do otherwise, here I stand, may God help me. Amen."[24] Through the gospel, God had saved Luther, made him righteous, and filled him with faith. That work of God kept Luther standing in that moment and enabled the Reformation to spread like wildfire. Apart from God's work here, countless Christians would have been kept without Scripture and the ability to understand that salvation is by faith and not by our works.

But what about us? Even if we accept on a heart level what the gospel does, how it works, and the difference it makes, and even if we have great moments of faith like Luther, we know that dark sins still lurk about in our hearts. In fact, the anxiety of our jobs, the pressures of family life, the chronic pain that throbs in our bodies, and the constant reminders of our sin can push Christians into a dark, dour, and distressed place. In short, many Christians live and act like they have nothing worth celebrating.

Luther fell into this trap of despair regularly. But in those moments, he forced himself to remember who the gospel was really about: "I simply taught, preached, and wrote God's Word; otherwise I did nothing. And while I slept, or drank Wittenberg beer with my friends Philip and Amsdorf, the Word so greatly weakened the papacy that no prince or emperor ever inflicted such losses upon it. I did nothing. The Word did everything."[25] Leave it to Luther to put it like that.

Luther, by grace, surely did more than nothing but he realized that in the grand scheme of things, Christ is the One who takes all the pressure, all the weight, and all the hope of the world upon his shoulders so that we, the redeemed, don't have to live as if it all rested upon us. Far too many Christians take themselves too seriously because we've forgotten who's done the heavy lifting. How then should we move forward?

First, we must make sure that we actually have the righteousness of God. All we need is need! Do you need forgiveness? Do you need to deal with your guilt? Are you spiritually dead? The good news is liberating! If you want the gospel, God is already at work within you. Seek him, for he has promised what you desire. The gospel is truly for all who believe that they don't meet God's standard but know that Christ does. And second, if you know that you have this righteousness, rejoice! In the midst of life's challenges and the gospel call to obedience, take time to stop and sing with joy. Find your Philip and Amsdorf as Luther did and celebrate God's ongoing work by laughing, feasting, and resting in Christ. God has done it. He's revealed the way to him. He's provided the righteousness your guilt and anxiety need. He's promised to provide for the path forward. This was Luther's light, and it can be yours as well.

"I am rough, boisterous, stormy, and altogether warlike, fighting against innumerable monsters and devils. I am born for the removing of stumps and stones, cutting away thistles and thorns, and clearing wild forests."

Martin Luther

Preface to Melanchthon's Commentary on Colossians

LEARNING FROM LUTHER

There is perhaps no other Reformer from whose pen you can better grasp his personality and persona than Luther. As one scholar notes, "Getting to know the real Martin Luther is not terribly difficult."[1] Certainly no study of the Reformation, or church history for that matter, is complete without the experience of reading Luther for yourself. Luther's writing is engaging, argumentative, often hilarious, sometimes cringe worthy, and even beautiful in its own blunt and boisterous way. No one could ever accuse Luther of hiding his true identity behind sanitized writing. For all those reasons, Luther is largely a joy to read.

Excerpts from Luther

Luther describing himself:

"I am an uncivilized fellow who has lived his life in the backwoods."[2]

"I cannot deny that I am more vehement than I ought to be."[3]

Luther on Scripture:

"For what solemn truth can the Scriptures still be concealing, now that the seals are broken, the stone rolled away from the door of the tomb, and the greatest of all mysteries brought to light—that Christ, God's Son, became man, that God is Three in One, that Christ suffered for us, and will reign forever? ... Take Christ from the Scriptures—and what more will you find in them? You see, then, that the entire content of the Scriptures has now been brought to light."[4]

"Take away assertions, and you take away Christianity ... I make it my invariable rule steadfastly to adhere to the sacred text in all that it teaches, and to assert that teaching ... [but] you [Erasmus] do not think it matters a scrap what anyone believes anywhere, so long as the world is at peace ... [But] leave us free to make assertions, and to find in assertions our satisfaction and delight ... The Holy Spirit is no Sceptic, and the things He has written in our hearts are not doubts or opinions, but assertions—surer and more certain than sense and life itself ... [But] your teaching is designed to induce us, out of consideration for Popes, princes and peace, to abandon and yield up for the present the sure Word of God. But when we abandon that, we abandon God, faith, salvation, and all Christianity."[5]

"For some years now, I have read through the Bible twice every year. If you picture the Bible to be a mighty tree and every word a little branch, I have shaken every one of these branches because I wanted to know what it was and what it meant."[6]

"If I profess with the loudest voice and clearest exposition every portion of the truth except precisely that little point which the world and the devil are at that moment attacking, I am not confessing Christ, however boldly I may be professing Christ. Where the battle rages, there the loyalty of the soldier is proved; to be steady on all the battlefield besides, is mere flight and disgrace if he flinches at that point."[7]

"The truth is that nobody who has not the Spirit of God sees a jot of what is in the Scriptures. All men have their hearts darkened, so that, even when they can discuss and quote all that is in Scripture, they do not understand or really know any of it. They do not believe in God, nor do they believe that they are God's creatures, nor anything else ... The Sprit is needed for the understanding of all Scripture and every part of Scripture ... Who will maintain that the town fountain does not stand in the light because the people down some alley cannot see it, while everyone in the square can see it?"[8]

Luther attacking his opponents:

"[Your writing was so] worthless and poor that my heart went out to you for having defiled your lovely, brilliant flow of language with such vile stuff ... it is like using gold or silver dishes to carry garden rubbish or dung ... You ooze Lucian from every pore ... This is weak stuff, Erasmus ... You tread like a cat on hot bricks."[9]

"A simple layman armed with Scripture is to be believed above a pope or council... For the sake of Scripture we should reject pope and council."[10]

"I certainly admit that there are some giddy preachers, who, from no religious or godly motive, but because they want applause, or hanker after novelty, or just cannot keep their mouths shut, talk the most frivolous nonsense."[11]

"In lying fashion you ignore what even children know... You think like this, 'As I am a crude ass, and do not read the books, so there is no one in the world who reads them; rather, when I let my braying heehaw, heehaw resound, or even let out a donkey's fart, then everyone will have to consider it pure truth.'"[12]

Luther on his marriage:

"[I got married to anger the Pope and to] make angels laugh and the devils weep."[13]

"[At first, it took me awhile to get used to] a pair of pig-tails lying beside me ... [but] I wouldn't give up my Katy for France or for Venice ... I shall die as one who loves and lauds marriage ... [Indeed] with the woman who has been joined to me by God I may jest [and] have fun."[14]

Comforting his wife as he died, Luther stated, "I have a caretaker who is better than you and all the angels; he lies in the cradle and rests on a virgin's bosom, and yet, nevertheless, he sits at the right hand of God, the almighty Father."[15]

Luther preaching the gospel in the story of Abraham and Isaac:

"The father raised the knife. The boy bared his throat. If God had slept an instant, the lad would have been dead. I could not have watched. The lad was as a sheep for the slaughter . . . But God was watching, and all the angels. The father raised his knife; the boy did not wince. The angel cried, 'Abraham, Abraham!' See how divine majesty is at hand in the hour of death. We say, 'In the midst of life we die.' God answers, 'Nay, in the midst of death, we live.'"[16]

Luther on music:

"I truly desire that all Christians would love and regard as worthy the lovely gift of music, which is a precious, worthy, and costly treasure given to mankind by God . . . In summa, next to the Word of God, the noble art of music is the greatest treasure in the world . . . A person who gives this some thought and yet does not regard music as a marvelous creation of God, must be a clodhopper indeed and does not deserve to be called a human being; he should be permitted to hear nothing but the braying of asses and the gruntings of hogs "[17]

Some of Luther's Ninety-Five Theses:

"1. When Our Lord and Master Jesus Christ said, 'Repent,' He willed the entire life of believers to be one of repentance."

"62. The true treasure of the church is the most holy gospel of the glory of and grace of God."

"94. Christians are to be exhorted to be diligent in following Christ, their Head, through penalties, death, and hell."[18]

Luther on the power of God and the power of man:

"Now, if I am ignorant of God's works and power, I am ignorant of God himself ... [and therefore] I cannot worship, praise, give thanks or serve him ... We need, therefore, to have in mind a clear-cut distinction between God's power and ours, and God's work and ours, if we would live a godly life ... all good in us is to be ascribed to God ... God's mercy alone works everything, and our will works nothing, but is rather the object of Divine working."[19]

"God foreknows nothing contingently, but that He foresees, purposes, and does all things according to His own immutable, eternal and infallible will. This bombshell knocks 'free-will' flat, and utterly shatters it ... For if you hesitate to believe, or are too proud to acknowledge, that God foreknows and wills all things, not contingently, but necessarily and immutably, how can you believe, trust and rely on His promises? When he makes promises, you ought to be out of doubt that He knows, and can and will perform, what He promises; otherwise, you will be accounting Him neither truthful nor faithful, which is unbelief, and the height of irreverence ... Not only should we be sure that God wills, and will execute His will, necessarily and immutably; we should glory in the fact ... or the Christian's chief and only comfort in every adversity lies in knowing that God does not lie, but brings all things to pass immutably, and that His will cannot be resisted, altered or impeded ... So man's will is like a beast standing between two riders. If God rides, it wills and goes where God wills . . . If Satan rides, it wills and goes where Satan wills. Nor may it choose to which rider it will run, or which it will seek . . . Hence it follows that 'free will' without God's grace is not free at all, but is the permanent prisoner and bond slave of evil, since it cannot turn itself to good."[20]

Luther on Christian liberties and temptation:

"Do not suppose that abuses are eliminated by destroying the object which is abused. Men can go wrong with wine and women. Shall we then prohibit and abolish women?"[21]

"Whenever . . . temptation comes to you beware not to dispute with the devil nor allow yourself to dwell on these lethal thoughts . . . By all means flee solitude, for he lies in wait most for those alone. This devil is conquered by despising and mocking him . . . seek the company of men or drink more, or joke and talk nonsense, or do some other merry thing. Sometimes we must . . . even sin a little to spite the devil, so that we leave him no place for troubling our consciences with trifles. We are conquered if we try too conscientiously not to sin at all . . . What other cause do you think I have for making merry so often, except that I wish to mock and harass the devil who is wont to mock and harass me."[22]

Luther on Romans 1:16–17:

"The Gospel is called the power of God in contradistinction to the power of man. The latter is the (supposed) ability by which he, according to his carnal opinion, obtains salvation by his own strength, and performs the things which are of the flesh. But this ability God, by the Cross of Christ, has utterly declared null and void, and He now gives us His power by which the spiritual—*the believer*—is empowered unto salvation ... God's righteousness is that by which we become worthy of His great salvation, or through which we alone are (accounted) righteous before Him ... Only the Gospel reveals the righteousness of God, that is, who is righteous, or how a person becomes righteous before God, namely, alone by faith, which trusts the Word of God ..."[23]

Recommended Luther Reading

While many episodes of Luther's life are well known and even capitalized upon in Hollywood, there is much more to be learned about the man. Because Luther allowed his end of the night, beer-in-hand, theological conversations to be recorded (these were known as "Table Talks") there is much for the interested student of history to learn.[24] In terms of biographies, Steven J. Lawson's *The Heroic Boldness of Martin Luther* is a great place to start. This work is short, accessible, and the next logical read for someone wanting to build upon the short look at Luther's life found in this work. While many modern biographies of Luther are overly critical, many older biographies gloss over Luther's various imperfections which is an equal disservice to both the imperfect reader and our Perfect Lord who chose to work through such a man as Luther. For this reason, I'd also recommend the fair, scholarly, and yet engaging work *The Legacy of Luther* edited by the late R.C. Sproul and Stephen J. Nichols. With contributions from top notch pastors and scholars, this book looks at nearly every aspect of the Reformer's life and teaching in easily accessible and clearly divided contributions. If you want to read more directly from Luther, you can find various writing compilations (such as John Dillenberger's *Martin Luther: Selections*

From His Writings) but I'd recommend reading a commentary of his, such as Romans, or diving straight into his classic work *The Bondage of The Will* (I recommend the translation by J.I. Packer and O.R. Johnson). This book is easy to start and enjoy even if the reader doesn't finish it. Luther addresses the core gospel issue of God's sovereignty in salvation by lambasting the reputable scholar Erasmus who emphasized the role of man in salvation instead. It is here that you will get a feel for Luther's genius, his love of the gospel of grace, and his relentless fury, dripped in humor, toward his opponents. Of course, Luther's Ninety-Five Theses are an easy and direct way to jump into his mind as well, although many are very rooted in the specific historical situation Luther found himself in. To get a feel for Luther's less formal remarks, the discerning reader can enjoy and laugh while reading Jim West's *Drinking with Calvin and Luther.* For those concerned with what is often, and with reason, considered Luther's greatest blemish—his harsh comments about his Jewish neighbors in later years—more insight can be found here.[25] Wherever you start, reading Luther is an absolutely unforgettable and worthwhile experience.

"And he gave the apostles, the prophets, the evangelists, the shepherds and teachers, to equip the saints for the work of ministry, for building up the body of Christ, until we all attain to the unity of the faith and of the knowledge of the Son of God, to mature manhood, to the measure of the stature of the fullness of Christ, so that we may no longer be children, tossed to and fro by the waves and carried about by every wind of doctrine, by human cunning, by craftiness in deceitful schemes. Rather, speaking the truth in love, we are to grow up in every way into him who is the head, into Christ, from whom the whole body, joined and held together by every joint with which it is equipped, when each part is working properly, makes the body grow so that it builds itself up in love."

Ephesians 4:11–16

CALVIN'S CALLING

In 1533, John Calvin's newfound belief in salvation by grace alone put his life in danger. He was forced to flee his native country of France and barely escaped arrest. This had been his sacrifice. This had been his big moment. Now, Calvin could get on with his life.

Calvin certainly had plans. He had settled in at the cozy Swiss town of Basal and decided to live a quiet life of scholarly study, stating, "The summit of my wishes, was the enjoyment of literary ease, with something of a free and honorable [calling] . . . I promised myself an easy, tranquil life."[1] But this was not to be Calvin's calling after all. Everything changed when Calvin was spotted by the wild reformer William Farel while passing through Geneva, Switzerland. Farel had heard of Calvin, had read some of his works, and openly confronted him, telling Calvin that he must abandon his quiet life and instead stay in Geneva as their pastor.

Here's how Calvin remembered the exchange: "Farel, who burned with extraordinary zeal to advance the Gospel, immediately strained every nerve to detain me . . . he proceeded to utter a threat that God would curse my retirement and the tranquility of my studies which I sought, if I should withdraw and refuse to give assistance [in this city], when the necessity was so urgent. I was so struck with fear that I desisted from the journey . . . [and stayed]."[2] All Calvin had wanted was a quiet life, but he was learning that God's calling was not his to choose.

Have you ever tried to control your calling? Have you ever tried to plan your life one way only to find that nothing would fall into place? Have you ever tried telling God how you want to serve him and what you want your relationship with him to look like? How has it worked out? Have you had more success in doing this than Calvin did? If we're honest, we all know what it's like to be thrown a curve ball from God. Throughout history, the Church at large has tried to pave its own way only to be corrected by God, as happened during the Reformation. Both the Church at large and individual Christians are prone to seeking an identity of our own making, not the one given to us by God.

And this is why we, like Calvin, need the Word of God. Specifically, we need to remember Ephesians 4:11–16,[3] which reminds us that we, the Church, are called to be the body of Christ. In fact, our ultimate purpose in life, our ultimate calling, is not ours to choose but God's to give because we, like Calvin, are not meant to be autonomous individuals but members of Christ's body. So what does it look like to stop fighting God's calling on our lives and to start living as the Word guides us?

Led in the Word

The book of Ephesians teaches that all Christians have equal value, dignity, and worth in Christ.[4] However, it also teaches that Christians have different callings from one another.[5] So who is it that God uses to lead his people? "And he gave the apostles, the prophets, the evangelists, the shepherds and teachers, to equip the saints . . ." (Ephesians 4:11–12). Christ has appointed certain Christians to lead the Church and therefore has provided the gifts required for this. In this Ephesians 4 list, we notice five titles. While there is some debate about the particulars of these titles,[6] we can break them down into three broad categories. The apostles and prophets were used by Christ to establish the Church before the New Testament was complete. The next title, evangelists, describes what we would call church planters and missionaries who take the gospel where it has not yet gone (or where it remains nominal). Finally, the last two titles, shepherds and teachers, are tied together in the original Greek as one office, which we call pastor. And so the picture that emerges is that of apostles and prophets starting the Church, evangelists spreading the church, and the shepherd teachers doing the daily teaching, equipping, leading, and growing of the Church.[7]

But why does this all matter? Simply put, the Church cannot survive without leadership. The term teacher describes one who can explain Scripture, who can provide spiritual food for the Church. The term shepherd, or pastor, is interchangeable in the New Testament with the words elder and overseer and refers to the one who leads and protects the Church.[8] Again, why is this crucial? "So that we may no longer be children, tossed to and fro by the waves and carried about by every wind of doctrine, by human cunning, by craftiness in deceitful schemes" (Ephesians 4:14). In this passage, the apostle Paul describes being rocked about in a boat by a raging sea and being spun by the wind to the point of dizziness in order to convey the danger of false teaching within the Church.[9] Apart from faithful teaching by pastors, the Church is likely to go dangerously astray.

The problem faced by the Church of Calvin's day was not an unwillingness to be led by pastors but rather an actual lack of true pastors. Many Catholic priests preached no more than once a year, often in Latin, and most had not actually read the Bible. Many Reformers reported that typical priests could not list the Ten Commandments or even describe the Sermon on the Mount. Those who did teach often viewed the Bible allegorically and thus ignored the history, grammar, and original intention of each text. Worse yet, most priests clearly did not know the gospel. The Church was being led by unsaved men.[10]

Through God's calling upon his life, Calvin realized that this was utterly unacceptable. Calvin sought to fix this in Geneva through several ways. First, Calvin preached nearly every day, offering up over two thousand sermons in his lifetime. Calvin then sought to supplement his preaching by writing at least one hundred thousand words a year, in commentaries, correspondence, and his famous and ever-expanding *Institutes of the Christians Religion*. Calvin's involvement in publishing further helped produce the imminently readable (at the time) Geneva Bible and Psalter for worship. Calvin didn't stop there. He dedicated himself to training future pastors three times a week, once sending out 150 new pastors in an eighteen-month period. Through Calvin's leadership, two thousand Reformed churches were planted in France, and missionaries were sent as far away as

Brazil.[11] This is the bar Calvin set for pastoral leadership in a local church.

If this is the gift of leadership that Christ has given his Church, what keeps us from embracing it today? Three trends need to be noted. First, our culture tends to be anti-authority. And, while self-sufficiency in the United States can be helpful in some regards, it can easily keep us from submitting to Church leaders and, worse yet, the Word of God. What is being called for here is not blind acceptance of pastoral authority but rather submission to leadership so far as it is faithful to God's Word. Is that a promise you've made at your local Church? Is that a standard you are holding your leaders to? These are important questions to consider.

The second trend to note is anti-intellectualism. There is a major strain within the Western Church that seeks entertainment, watered down, feel-good sermons, emotional highs, and nothing that requires serious thinking and study. This trend keeps Christians from growing in their knowledge of the truth, which is vital for the Christian life. Are you actively engaging the Word through serious study both on a personal level and under the leadership of a pastor who does the same?

The final trend to be aware of is what might be dubbed anti-applicationism. There is another major strain within the Church in the United States, especially in Reformed circles, that loves to learn difficult and challenging doctrines but fails and is even resistant to applying such knowledge to their hearts, their private lives, major social issues, and everyday experiences. This is dead knowledge and it cripples a Christian's testimony and relationship with the Lord. Are you taking your knowledge of the truth, led by a pastor who is doing the same, and applying it to daily life? The truth is, whenever we push back on faithful authority, on an intellec- tual study of Scripture, or real-life application, we are trying to control our calling as Christians. What we need instead is to be lead by faithful pastors who know, study, teach, and ap- ply the Word.

Equipped for Ministry

Is it only pastors then that do ministry? This common conception couldn't be further from the truth. The whole church is called to ministry. Before the Reformation, nearly all ministry was carried out by full-time clergy. However, the Reformation not only rediscovered the biblical truth that a lo- cal church is led by multiple leaders (such as elders who have different day jobs) but also that these leaders seek to "equip the saints for the work of ministry, for the building up of the body of Christ" (Ephesians 4:12).[12] Who do pastors and teach- ers (and elders) equip? The saints. Who are the saints? Biblically speaking, saints refers to all Christians, to all true believers.[13] Thus, the whole Church is to be trained up for ministry: "every Christian has a work of ministry."[14] The rea- son that teachers are mentioned first is not because they are the only ones who do ministry, or even that they are the most important ministry workers, but simply because it's their job to start that process in the Church. The Reformation not only produced better teachers for the Church but it also gave con- gregations what they needed to join in on ministry.

So what kind of ministry is the Church to do? The Church is called to present the whole gospel to all people. Instead of being tossed about and blown around, the Church is to be equipped by teachers so that "the whole body, joined and held together by every joint with which it is equipped, when each part is working properly," speaks the truth in love (Ephesians 4:15–16). There are two things that must be noticed here. First, this body is comprised of all the members of the Church, meaning everyone is needed. Second, the gospel is shared with the world by speaking the truth (with words) in love (demonstrated by actions), and this requires each and every part of the body.[15] In other words, sharing the whole gospel (in word and deed) requires the whole Church using all of its gifts. Calvin put it well when he said, "No member of the body exists to serve itself, rather it puts its abilities to use for the good of our neighbors."[16]

Calvin learned that the Church had to live as the hands and feet of Jesus if the gospel he preached was to be believed. Calvin was blessed by generous donors and a team of deacons who led the whole church in meeting the material needs of others. This group helped find work for unemployed men, apprenticed young boys, supported widows, fostered orphans, provided money so that refugees could be reunited with family members, provided clothing, firewood, and medical treatment for the needy, and transcribed Calvin's sermons so that more people could be reached. [17] Once again, the standard for Church-wide ministry was set high in Geneva.

But what about you? Have you bought in? Are you using your gifts in the ministry of your local Church? Are you blessing your neighbors through your daily work? Here's a good set of questions to help Christians get started. First, do you know your gifts? Do you know how you function best in the body? Have you spent time thinking about this? Have you asked this question to others who know you well? This is a great place to begin. Second, if you've done this, are you using your gifts daily? Do they shine both in your work and in relationship to your Church? If not, why? What's keeping you

back? Is there a disconnect between your day job and ministry with the Church? Third, if you are doing the above, are you
also recognizing and helping to utilize the gifts of others? Are
you encouraging those with different gifts? And finally, if you
are doing that, are you submitting the use of your gifts to the
authority of the Word, the leaders of your church, and relying
on the power of Christ to serve? No matter who you are,
there's somewhere in this list where we all can grow.[18]

United in Christ

Biblical leadership and church-wide ministry sounds
good on paper. And then we face the realities of living as broken and sinful people in a broken and sinful world. Thus, the
call to unity within the Church is easier said than done. If we
claim to be growing in the Word, serving our neighbors, and
yet fail to do so as a loving and unified Church body, we've
missed it all. For we are to seek "the building up of the body
of Christ, until we all attain to the unity of the faith and of the
knowledge of the Son of God, to mature manhood, to the
measure of the stature of the fullness of Christ" (Ephesians
4:12–13). We miss the end goal if we love outsiders but not
each other. If the Church doesn't love the Church, those who
are saved have no forever family to lovingly welcome them;
rather, they are thrust into a warzone. That is not the goal of
gospel ministry. But what kind of unity should we seek? It
can't be based on politics, culture, racial identity, economic
factors, or even shared interests. It can only be found in
Christ.

This is certainly difficult at best. It is hard to love *everyone*
within the body of Christ—especially when we've been
burned, offended, or found ourselves in bitter disagreements.

Early in his ministry, Calvin was told not to withhold communion from those who refused to repent of their sins, even though the Bible clearly teaches to do so.[19] Calvin saw this form of discipline as essential to the unity, purity, and ongoing love of the Church and wouldn't back down. While Calvin was right in principle, the way he handled the situation was not perfect. In the end, he was shockingly stripped of his position and told to leave Geneva within three days.[20] After all that he'd sacrificed, all that he'd done, he was tossed to the curb. If anyone had a reason to be done with the Church, it was Calvin. However, three years later, Geneva asked him to return. Personally, Calvin hated the idea, dramatically telling a friend, "It would be far better to perish once for all than to be tormented again in that torture chamber."[21] Even so, Calvin knew this wasn't up to him. Because his love for the Church was rooted in his love of Christ, Calvin returned, saying, "But when I remember that I am not my own, I offer up my heart, presented as a sacrifice to the Lord . . . Therefore I submit my will and affections, subdued and held fast, to the obedience of God."[22]

Love for Christ is the key to unity within the Church. Listen to how Paul completes the picture of the Church: "until we all attain to the unity of the faith and of the knowledge of the Son of God, to mature manhood, to the measure of the stature of the fullness of Christ . . . Rather, speaking the truth in love, we are to grow up in every way into him who is the head, into Christ" (Ephesians 4:13–15). Our unity is not just based on a shared theology of Christ, but a deep and intimate knowledge of the Son of God, comparable to the way a husband knows his wife. Because he loved Christ and knew that the Church was his bride, Calvin said, "We must not thoughtlessly forsake the Church because of any petty dissensions. Indeed, [referring to the Church as a mother], there is no other way to enter into life unless this mother conceives us in her womb, gives us birth, nourishes us at her breast, and lastly, unless she keeps us under her care and guides us until eternity. Our weakness does not allow us to be dismissed from her school until we have been pupils all our lives. Furthermore, away from her bosom one cannot hope [for the spiritual benefits of Christ] ... God's favor and the especial witness of spiritual life are limited to his flock, so that it is always disastrous to leave the church."[23] Because Calvin had been called by Christ, he was called to the Church.

But oh how much easier it is to set our own calling. We're not only at times disillusioned with the Church and our pastors, but we struggle with the brokenness of this world and our bodies, the sin that lives within, and the false promise of an easier life if only we'd free ourselves from submitting to the Church, the sacrifices required by ministry, and the patience and love required for unity. Calvin certainly struggled mightily. His body was wrecked with hook worms, perpetual kidney and gall stones, migraines, insomnia, a diseased trachea which caused him to spit blood, pleurisy, hemorrhoids, internal abscesses, and arthritis.[24] And Calvin also struggled with his heart. He was irritable, had a short temper, was proud (he knew that he was always the smartest man in any room, and he truly was), he held grudges and was slow to forgive, he couldn't handle criticism, he could be reclusive and out of touch, and was often unsympathetic to others.[25] Even so, he knew that our hope was not in our perfection but in keeping our eyes on the grace of the Lord who calls us. Calvin put it like this: "I'm not saying that the conduct of a Christian will breathe nothing but pure gospel, although this should be desired and pursued. I'm not, in other words, talking about gospel perfection ... If that were the case, everyone would be excluded from the church ... Indeed, most of us are so oppressed with weakness that we make little progress—staggering, limping, and crawling on the ground. But let us move forward according to the measure of our resources [in Christ] ... What I'm saying is this: Let us fix our eyes on the goal and sole object of our pursuit."[26] Brothers and sisters, like Calvin, may we know our Savior and because of that, may we pursue our calling as a Church by his grace.

"Wherever we see the Word of God sincerely preached and heard, wherever we see the sacraments administered according to the institution of Christ, there we cannot have any doubt that the Church of God has some existence, since his promise cannot fail ..."

John Calvin
Institutes of the Christian Religion

LEARNING FROM CALVIN

Reading from Calvin couldn't be any more different than reading Luther. Calvin characteristically writes with restraint: "Calvin was not a man to lay bare his soul. His innate reserve as well as his objective outlook kept him from it."[1] As a result, everything Calvin writes has been measured, evaluated, often rewritten, and polished. Nevertheless, Calvin's writing demonstrates thoughtfulness, exceptional logic, clarity, and elegance. Many would agree that Calvin represents one of the greatest minds in history: "To read Calvin is to be in the hands of a master of language."[2] That being said, don't let Calvin's seriousness or intellect scare you away. As Bruce Gordon notes, "The enduring [and inaccurate] image of Calvin as an unyielding, moralistic and stone-faced tyrant who rejected all the pleasures of life has been his opponent's greatest victory."[3] In truth, Calvin's writing, like the man, is often pastoral, vividly clear, and, as can be seen in good modern translations, down to earth.

Excerpts from Calvin

Calvin on the gospel, grace, and Christ:

"I offer my heart to you, O Lord, promptly and sincerely."[4]

"When at first we taste the Gospel we indeed see God's smiling countenance turned towards us, but at a distance: the more the knowledge of true religion grows in us, by coming as it were nearer, we behold God's favor more clearly and more familiarly."[5]

"[We must tell a man] that he was alienated from God by sin, an heir of wrath, liable to the punishment of eternal death, excluded from all hope of salvation, a total stranger to the blessing of God, a slave to Satan, a captive under the yoke of sin, and, in a word, condemned to and already involved in, a horrible destruction; that, in this situation, Christ interposed as an intercessor; that He has taken upon Himself and suffered the punishment which by the righteous judgement of God impended over all sinners; that by His blood He has expiated those crimes which make them odious to God; that by this expiation God the Father has been duly satisfied and atoned; that by this intercessor His wrath has been appeased; that this is the foundation of peace between God and men; that this is the bond of His benevolence towards them." [6]

"No one has made much progress in the school of Christ who doesn't look forward joyfully both to his death and the day of his final resurrection."[7]

"[Christ] sits on high that from thence He may shed forth His power upon us, that He may animate us with spiritual life, that he may sanctify us by His Spirit, that He may adorn His Church with a variety of graces, and defend it by His protection from every calamity, that by the strength of His hand, He may restrain the fierce enemies of His Cross and of our salvation; finally, that He may retain all power in heaven and on earth, till he shall have overthrown all His enemies, who are ours also, and shall have completed the building up of his Church. And this is the true state of His kingdom, this the power which the Father has conferred upon Him, till He completes the last act by coming to judge the living and the dead."[8]

"Not only, therefore, does He declare that the love of God is free, but likewise that God displayed it in the riches, the extraordinary and preeminent riches of His grace. It deserves notice also that the name of Christ is repeated; for no grace, no love, is to be expected by us from God except through His mediation."[9]

"[In the Catholic Church] They certainly preached of Thy mercy towards men, but confided it to those who could show that they deserved it. What is more, they placed this deserving in the righteousness of works, so that he alone was received into Thy favor who reconciled himself to Thee by works."[10]

"To sum up everything in a word: The cross of Christ finally triumphs in believer's hearts—over the devil, the flesh, sin, and the wicked—when their eyes are turned to the power of the resurrection."[11]

Calvin on the death of his wife:

"You know well how tender, or rather soft, my mind is. Had not a powerful self-control been given to me, I could not have borne up so long. And truly, mine is no common source of grief. I have been bereaved of the best companion of my life, of who, had it been so ordained, would have willingly shared not only my poverty but even my death. During her life she was the faithful helper of my ministry . . . throughout the whole course of her illness [she was] more anxious about her children than about herself."[12]

Calvin on the Church:

"Out of a variety [of gifts] arises unity in the church, as the various tones in music produce sweet melody."[13]

"In short, the government of the church, by the ministry of the word, is not a contrivance of men, but an appointment made by the Son of God. As his own unalterable law, it demands our assent. They who reject or despise this ministry offer insult and rebellion to Christ its Author . . . Another inference is, that no man will be fit or qualified for so distinguished an office who has not been formed and moulded by the hand of Christ himself. To Christ we owe it that we have ministers of the gospel, that they abound in necessary qualifications, that they execute the trust committed to them. All, all is his gift . . . The church is the common mother of all the godly, which bears, nourishes, and brings up children of God, kings and peasants alike; and this is done by the ministry. Those who neglect or despise this order choose to be wiser than Christ. Woe to the pride of such men!"[14]

"Without mutual love, the health of the body cannot be maintained. Through the members, as canals, is conveyed from the head all that is necessary for the nourishment of the body. While this connection is upheld, the body is alive and healthy ... No increase is advantageous, which does not bear a just proportion to the whole body. That man is mistaken who desires his own separate growth. If a leg or arm should grow to a prodigious size, or the mouth be more fully distended, would the undue enlargement of those parts be otherwise than injurious to the whole frame? In like manner, if we wish to be considered members of Christ, let no man be anything for himself, but let us all be whatever we are for the benefit of each other. This is accomplished by love."[15]

"We might say, 'I have done this, and I have done that; is it not enough?' What? What are the terms upon which God has called us to His service? Is it just for one act, or two, and thereafter He has given us leave to have a rest? Not at all; it is that we may dedicate ourselves to Him in life and in death, and that we may be His entirely."[16]

Calvin on Italy:

"I only went to Italy, that I might have the pleasure of leaving it."[17]

Calvin on enjoying life:

"We are nowhere forbidden to laugh, or to be satisfied with food ... or to be delighted with music, or to drink wine ... it is permissible to use wine not only for necessity, but also to make us merry ... [that we might] feel a livelier gratitude to God."[18]

"The use of gifts of God cannot be wrong, if they are directed to the same purpose for which the Creator himself has created and destined them ... For he has made the earthly blessings for our benefit, and not for our harm ... [God's] intention [is] not only to provide for our needs, but likewise our pleasure, and for our delight."[19]

Calvin on the importance of the Word

"[We should not] allow ourselves to investigate God anywhere but in His sacred Word, or to form any ideas of Him but such as are agreeable to His Word, or to speak anything concerning Him but what is derived from the same Word."[20]

Calvin's frustrations with unqualified pastors:

"Our colleagues are rather a hindrance than a help to us: they are rude and self-conceited, have no zeal, and less learning. But, worst of all, I cannot trust them, even though I very much wish that I could ... I bear with them, however, or rather I humor them with the utmost leniency ... But, in the long run, the sore needs a severer remedy. I shall do my utmost to avoid disturbing the peace of the church with our quarrels by every means I can think of."[21]

"Such nominal Christians demonstrate their knowledge of Christ to be false and offensive no matter how eloquently and loudly they talk about the gospel. For true doctrine is not a matter of the tongue, but of life; neither is Christian doctrine grasped only by the intellect and memory, as truth grasped in other fields of study. Rather, doctrine is rightly received when it takes possession of the entire soul and finds a dwelling place and shelter in the most intimate affections of the heart.

So let such people stop lying, or let them prove themselves worthy disciples of Christ, their teacher."[22]

Calvin on suffering:

"We will rejoice when He considers us worthy to suffer disgrace for His name ... What then? Though innocent and clear of conscience, we might be stripped of our resources by the wickedness of the ungodly, and so reduced to poverty in the view of men—but before God in heaven our riches are thereby truly increased. We might be thrust out of our homes, but thereby we are drawn more intimately into God's household. We might be harassed and despised, but thereby we drive deeper roots into Christ. We might be branded with disgrace and dishonor, but thereby we gain a more honorable rank in the kingdom of God. We might be slaughtered, but thereby a door unto the blessed life is opened to us."[23]

Calvin on himself:

"But, alas, my desires and my zeal, if I may so describe it, have been so cold and flagging that I am conscious of imperfections in all that I am and do."[24]

"For although I follow [King] David at a great distance, and come far short of equaling him ... I still feel myself tarnished with the contrary vices. Yet, if I have anything in common with him, I have no hesitation in comparing myself to him. In reading the instances of his faith, patience, fervor, zeal and integrity, it has, as it ought, drawn from me unnumbered groans and sighs that I am so far from approaching them. It has, however, been of very great advantage to me to behold in him, as in a mirror, both the commencement of my calling and the continued course of my actions, so that I know more certainly that whatever [he] suffered was exhibited to me by God as an example for imitation."[25]

Calvin on predestination:

"[I] live and die in this faith which [God] has bestowed on me, having no other hope nor refuge than in His predestination, upon which all my salvation is founded."[26]

Recommend Calvin Reading

While Calvin is not the easiest Reformer to read, perhaps no Reformer has left behind a better, clearer, and simpler book to start with. Calvin's *Little Book On The Christian Life*, especially in the new and absolutely outstanding translation by Aaron Denlinger and Burk Parson, is simply a must read. Beyond this, Calvin has left behind his magisterial work *The Institutes of The Christian Religion*, which is truly a work of art and yet not for the faint hearted. If reading through them is too intimidating, the reader is encouraged to use them as references, reading particular sections and dealing with particular topics one at a time. Perhaps the best way to start this is through using *Knowing God and Ourselves: Reading Calvin's Institutes Devotionally* by David Calhoun. This will guide and encourage your first crack into Calvin's masterpiece. Calvin's commentaries and sermons, covering most of the books of the Bible, are also of top quality and well worth consulting. Readers will quickly discover that Calvin often applies the text to the specific issues of the Reformation in such detail that modern readers may need to skim ahead. In terms of reading about Calvin, the short yet solid *The Expository Genius of John Calvin* by Steven J. Lawson is commended as well as the short, older, slightly more scholarly, yet truly more biographic *Portrait of Calvin* by T.H.L Parker that has recently come back into print. For a full-length treatment of Calvin, Bruce Gordon's *Calvin* is the standard bearer. This book is rightfully critical of Calvin where it should be yet understanding, appreciative, and fair at all times. The book reveals neither an air-brushed hero nor a cranky villain, but rather a real, talented, imperfect, yet incredible man who changed the history of the world. This is a hefty read but worth every minute invested. For those concerned with what is often regarded, inaccurately, as Calvin's greatest blemish, the Servetus incident, Gordon's treatment is suburb.[27] While many are intimidated by Calvin, this attitude is neither necessary nor helpful. Starting with his shorter works and shorter biographies, modern readers can find much to their profit and enjoyment.

"When Jesus had spoken these words, he lifted up his eyes to heaven, and said, 'Father, the hour has come; glorify your Son that the Son may glorify you, since you have given him authority over all flesh, to give eternal life to all whom you have given him. And this is eternal life, that they know you, the only true God, and Jesus Christ whom you have sent. I glorified you on earth, having accomplished the work that you gave me to do. And now, Father, glorify me in your own presence with the glory that I had with you before the world existed. I have manifested your name to the people whom you gave me out of the world. Yours they were, and you gave them to me, and they have kept your word . . . I am praying for them . . . And I am no longer in the world, but they are in the world . . . keep them in your name, which you have given me, that they may be one, even as we are one. While I was with them, I kept them in your name, which you have given me. I have guarded them, and not one of them has been lost . . . and the world has hated them because they are not of the world, just as I am not of the world. I do not ask that you take them out of the world, but that you keep them from the evil one. They are not of the world, just as I am not of the world . . . As you sent me into the world, so I have sent them into the world . . . I do not ask for these only, but also for those who will believe in me through their word, that they may all be one, just as you, Father, are in me, and I in you, that they also may be in us, so that the world may believe that you have sent me . . . Father, I desire that they also, whom you have given me, may be with me where I am, to see my glory that you have given me because you loved me before the foundation of the world . . . I will continue to make it known, that the love with which you have loved me may be in them, and I in them.'"

Excerpt from John 17

KNOX'S ANCHOR

His muscles seared with pain, his lungs desperately gasped for air, and his stomach ached from starvation. Even so, the whip came, and Knox rowed on. The castle in which John Knox pastored had fallen to Catholic forces in 1547 and Knox was given a punishment considered just one step above execution: working as a galley slave upon a French naval ship. For nineteen months, Knox endured forced labor, limited rations, and iron shackles as he and four other men rowed a fifty-foot oar together.[1]

To make matters worse, Knox's captors taunted him and his faith, thrusting idols and images into his face, demanding that he worship them. He always refused, and on one occasion threw a painted image of Mary into the waves declaring, "Such an idol is accursed . . . Let our Lady now save herself . . . She is light enough. Let her learn to swim."[2] Knox's bold behavior, fitting his reputation as a fiery Scotsman, brought beatings and inspired further protestation by other Protestant Scottish slaves. In all of this, Knox had only been a Christian for less than five years and a pastor less than one.

And he was facing what would be one of many severe tests not only to his life but also his faith. How would he endure?

When the storms of suffering come, what do you cling to? Where is your security in life when everything goes wrong? We've all been here, and if we haven't, we will be. The call that no one ever wants eventually comes. There's been an accident, a lay-off, a foreclosure, a terminal diagnosis, a child in trouble, a marriage on the rocks, crashing stocks, or a drought that will not end. We try to patch these things as best as we can. But sometimes our savings account, past success, good health, or strong work ethic simply can't fix the problem. What then do you cling to? Even if it's God, what about God can you cling to if you're wracked with doubt, if you've fallen into sin, or if your faith has been neglected?

In storms such as this, John Knox would turn where we all should turn, the Word of God. Specifically, Knox sought out John 17,[3] a passage he named as his "first anchor."[4] Knox chose this phrase because it described the primary and most import line of safety afforded to an ancient ship. And as this passage is studied, it's easy to see the connection. In John 17, Jesus prays not only for his twelve disciples but for all Christians throughout history[5] asking that they "also may be in us [The Father and Son], so that the world may believe that you have sent me" (John 17:21). Knox knew that all Christians needed to believe that they were forever connected to the Son, like an anchor, if they wanted to survive the storms of suffering found throughout this life.

Connected to the Son, before This Life

As we struggle with suffering, it becomes easy to hyper-focus upon present pain. Knox, however, found great comfort in knowing that Christ shifts our focus first to eternity past. Before suffering on the cross, Christ looked backwards: "And now, Father, glorify me in your presence with the glory that I had with you before the world existed" (John 17:5). As the Son prays to the Father, he fixates not on present pain or future questions but on the history of his relationship with the Father. We must remember that the Son's story does not start with his incarnation, ministry, and the cross but with a loving and intimate relationship with the Father going back into eternity.[6] This defines who the Son is, what his purpose is, and explains why he can have hope. It's all rooted in an eternal relationship.

From this perspective, the Son also shows us our place in eternity past. For Knox, the best news of John 17 was not simply that the Son had an eternal relationship with the Father but that, through our connection to the Son, we do as well.[7] "Father . . . you have given [me] authority over all flesh, to give eternal life to all whom you have given [me] . . . I have manifested your name to the people whom you gave me out of the world. Yours they were, and you gave them to me, and they have kept your word" (John 17:1–2, 6). Christians must see that they are saved because they belong to the Father who has chosen them eternally and has now given them to the Son. The reason a Christian is saved—indeed the reason a Christian knows God—is because of God's choice in eternity past apart from anything they have done or will do.[8] Christians eternally belong to God. And so, this defines who we are, what our purpose is, and why we too can have hope in suffering. Again, it's all rooted in an eternal relationship.

This eternal relationship means that our faith story begins far before we ever profess faith. Before Knox believed in the gospel, God was planning his faith and preparing him.

Born and baptized in the Catholic Church, Knox learned early on to appreciate the power and importance of the Church.[9] Born as the second male in his family, Knox did not inherit his father's business (which he would have preferred) and instead had to find another job.[10] This led Knox toward training for a career within the Catholic Church. Through his priestly training, Knox learned to love reading, singing, studying, and debating Scripture even though he was not yet saved.[11] When Knox failed to quickly rise through the ranks of the Church, he switched to a career as a notary, or country lawyer, where his personal motto "Not to bear false witness" would later be a truth that defined his ministry of bearing witness to the truth of the gospel no matter the cost.[12] Through connections in this job, Knox finally met the man who would teach him the gospel and then train him to preach.[13] God was at work far before Knox believed.

How can knowing that we eternally belong to God help us? Knox put it like this: "There is no way more proper to build and establish faith, than when we hear and undoubtedly do believe that our election . . . consisteth not in ourselves, but in the eternal and immutable good pleasure of God. And that in such firmity that it can not be overthrown."[14] Knox is saying that Christians are eternally, and graciously, secure in the Son from eternity past. In light of this, no type of suffering, temptation, or weakness of our own can change God's plans for us. Through our connection to Christ, God always gets the final word on us. And this, indeed, is the good news of the gospel.

Connected to the Son, in This Life

In John 17, Christ mentions two dangers that all Christians face: "I have given them your word, and the world has hated them because they are not of the world, just as I am not of the world. I do not ask that you take them out of the world, but that you keep them from the evil one" (John 17:14–15). First, Christians must deal with the world. Believers serve a different king, have a different agenda, and live out a different way of life than the rest of the world.[15] Christ was hated for this and Christians will be as well.[16] This hatred takes many forms including mockery, economic, political, and social disadvantages, and persecution. The second danger we face is Satan.[17] While Christ defeated Satan on the cross, this enemy is still a formidable opponent who has focused his destructive efforts upon Christ's followers. This too takes many forms including temptation and suffering. And yet, there's good news for us in Christ's prayer: "Holy Father, keep them in your name, which you have given me, that they may be one, even as we are one. While I was with them, I kept them in your name, which you have given me. I have guarded them, and not one of them has been lost." (John 17:11–12). Just as the Son preserved the disciples in the midst of dangers, he prays that through our connection to him, we might also be presently preserved.

The Son however, has more in mind than present protection. He seeks more importantly to direct us. If safety was the goal, Christ would simply take all the Christians out of the world or return immediately to judge the world. Instead, Christ preserves us for a reason. "I do not ask that you take them out of the world, but that you keep them from the evil one. They are not of the world, just as I am not of the world.

Sanctify them in the truth; your word is truth. As you sent me into the world, so I have sent them into the world. And for their sake I consecrate myself, that they also may be sanctified in truth" (John 17:15–16). The Son preserves us so that we might carry out his mission.[18] This requires not absence from the world or imitation of the world but a life-giving witness in the world.[19] We must stay, engage, and love the world as we are personally transformed by the truth. This is only possible because of our present connection to the Son.

If anyone ever had a reason to avoid their place of calling in this world, it was Knox. As he ministered in Scotland, he narrowly survived the execution of his mentor, a siege of St. Andrews Castle, and life as a galley slave.[20] Even after his release, Knox couldn't safely return to the land ruled by Mary Queen of Scots and so worked in England for a time as an army chaplain before Bloody Mary took the throne and forced him to flee to Calvin's Geneva.[21] Once he finally got away, Knox had great reasons for wanting to keep his distance from Scotland. Not only did life in Geneva feel like paradise, but Knox also recognized his weakness. Knox was permanently and physically weakened by his time as a slave and he was truly terrified of either dying as a martyr or worse, recanting his faith under torture. Knox confessed this to friends saying, "I quake, I fear, and tremble."[22] Even so, John 17 taught Knox that this life wasn't about escaping difficulties and so, with both faith and fear, Knox returned to Scotland. With growing threats against his life, he preached tirelessly with passion and truth, even before the face of his murderous Queen. Through Knox's obedience, the Scottish Reformation was kick-started.[23]

Knox knew his purpose and also knew that the Son would keep him as long as needed. Do you know your purpose? We all pray for safety and success, but do we connect our desire for God's protection with the mission he has for us? All Christians are called to love God and minister to this world. What does that look like for you? We are not connected to the Son's preserving presence in this life simply for our own comfort. We are here for a purpose. We need to embrace that purpose and burn with passion for it like Knox.

Connected to the Son, after This Life

Christ ends his prayer in John 17 with his eyes upon the future. "Father, I desire that they also, whom you have given me, may be with me where I am, to see my glory that you have given me because you loved me." (John 17:24). The Son prays that after this life, after our mission is complete, we'll be brought into his heavenly presence. It is in this place that we'll see the miracle of transformation and resurrection. Indeed, we'll finally and fully see the splendor, majesty, and blinding brilliance of heavenly glory as the true King and his redeemed stand exalted in the presence of the Father to worship and to await a New Heaven and a New Earth.[24] And it's our connection to the Son that leads to this moment. What a gift to be inseparably connected to the glory of the Son.

But there's more than glory here. While Knox was known for letting his zeal for the glory of Christ lead the way in his thundering sermons about repentance and uncompromising obedience, John 17 led him back to grace. "O righteous Father, even though the world does not know you, I know you, and these know that you have sent me. I made known to them your name, and I will continue to make it known, that the love with which you have loved me may be in them, and I in them" (John 17:25–26). The Son's prayer ends with a request that the deepest longing of every human heart might be met—that God, who is love, would again dwell with his people in unde-filed, uninterrupted, and unending love. Don't miss the connection. The Son is praying that the Father's perfect and infinite love for him would be given to those who are saved. This deep truth is the anchor of John 17 and all of Scripture. Our past, present, and future connection to Christ points to the everlasting love and grace of the Father for us.

The best example of the tender love of the Son breaking out in the stubborn, faithful, and flawed Scotsman Knox comes in a private letter that Knox sent his mother-in-law, who was wrestling with doubt about her salvation and guilt over sin. "Remember, mother, that Jesus the Son of God came not in the flesh to call the just, but to call sinners . . . with hope of mercy and forgiveness of God by the redemption that is in Christ's blood . . . Your imperfection shall have no power to damn you, for Christ's perfection is reputed to be yours by faith, which you have in his blood."[25] What tenderness and truth the love of the Son imparted in Knox!

While Knox undoubtedly matured during his life, his struggle with sin continued until his death. Indeed, the more that is learned about Knox, the more his imperfections be-come clear. He could be overly negative, struggled to forgive others, had a short temper, a sharp and critical tongue, and a hard time with apologies and accepting blame. He often con-fused political enemies for religious ones, sometimes equated minor theological disagreements with heresy, was known to ignore wise counsel from trusted friends, and sometimes put forth arguments that were far from consistent.[26] While all of this could make a modern reader appreciate him less, it should indeed bring us to appreciate John 17, his spiritual an-chor, all the more. More than anything else, Knox believed that these verses were prayed by the Son for him and every other future believer in mind: "I do not ask for these only but also for those who will believe in me through their word, that they may all be one, just as you, Father, are in me, and I in you, that they also may be in us, so that the world may believe that you have sent me" (John 17: 20–21).

Knox believed that even he had been connected to the Son back into eternity past, elected by the Father based on grace alone. He believed that even he was connected to the Son in this life so that he'd be protected to do what he was called to do. Most importantly, he believed that even he was connected to the Son in eternity future, that even he would see the glory of the King and bask in the love of the Father. Because of this, on his deathbed, Knox asked his wife to go back to this first anchor, John 17, and read it to him one last time.[27]

Knox's election, justification, progressive sanctification, and future glorification (as described in John 17), were a product of grace through his connection to the Son.[28] Knox confessed, "In youth, middle age, and now, after many battles, I find nothing in me but vanity and corruption. For in quietness I am negligent, in trouble impatient, tending to desperation, and in the mean state, I am so carried away with [political worries] that alas O Lord, it draws me away from your presence."[29] Can you see yourself in Knox? Can you see your worries, your insecurities, your vanities, your political idolatries, your struggle with pride, your difficulties with forgiveness, and your reliance upon health, finances, power, control, and gifts? There is but one hope. Turn your eyes to that faithful anchor of the Son who is the same yesterday, today, and forever more and who has called you, kept you, and who awaits you in glory, all based upon grace alone!

"I sought neither preeminence, glory, nor riches; my honor was that Jesus Christ should reign."

John Knox

Epistle to the Inhabitants of Newcastle and Berwick

LEARNING FROM KNOX

Of the three Reformers covered in this work, the inability to hear Knox preach leaves the modern reader at the greatest disadvantage. Where Knox lagged behind Calvin in intellect, he surely made up for in oratory.[1] Even still, Knox wrote a great deal throughout his life and his writing has "a strong sense of the picturesque and an even stronger sense of the ludicrous. He had great powers of expression; he was not only articulate, he was an artist."[2] While Knox is often remembered for his most extreme and volatile writing, accurately referred to as political "thunderclaps," most of his work exhibits "the art of simple written communication ... [filled with] passion, tenderness, and theological clarity."[3] C.S. Lewis even noted Knox's humor and compassion.[4] Indeed, when Knox's personal correspondence is read, especially to his female supporters, an entirely different side of Knox is revealed.[5] In truth, Knox must be widely read to fully appreciate the scope not only of his concerns but also of his personality.

Excerpts from Knox

Knox on preaching:

"O Lord Eternal, move and govern my tongue to speak the truth."[6]

"The Scriptures of God are my only foundations and substance in all matters of weight and importance."[7]

"I have never once feared the devil, but I tremble every time I enter the pulpit."[8]

"The end I proposed in all my preaching was to instruct the ignorant, to confirm the weak, to comfort the consciences of those who were humbled under the sense of their sins, and bear down, with the threatening of God's judgments, such as were proud and rebellious . . . to gain [them all] to Christ."[9]

"I have learned plainly and boldly to call wickedness by its terms, a fig a fig, and a spade a spade."[10]

"It has pleased His merciful providence, to make me, among others, a simple soldier, and witness-bearer, unto men."[11]

"Christ in every verb, in every noun, in every adverb, in every adjective, in every participle—Christ is in every syntactical device in all of Scripture."[12]

Knox against his enemies:

"O God Eternal! Hast thou laid none other burden upon our backs than Jesus Christ laid bare by His Word? Then who hath burdened us with all these ceremonies, prescribed fasting, compelled chastity, unlawful vows, invocations of saints, with the idolatry of the Mass? The Devil, the Devil, brethren, invented all these burdens to depress imprudent men to perdition."[13]

"After the death of this most virtuous Prince, of whom the godless people of England for the most part were not worthy, Satan intended nothing less than that the light of Jesus Christ utterly to have been extinguished within the whole Isle of Britain; for after him was raised up, in God's hot displeasure, that idolatress Jezebel, mischievous Mary, of the Spaniard's blood, cruel persecutrix of God's people."[14]

"Madam, as right religion took neither original strength nor authority from worldly princes, but from the Eternal God alone, so are not subjects bound to frame their religion according to the appetites of their princes."[15]

Knox on prayer:

"Prayer is an earnest and familiar talking with God, to whom we declare all our miseries, whose support and help we implore and desire in our adversities, and whom we laud and praise for our benefits received. So that prayer contains the exposition of our sorrows, the desire of God's defense, and the praising of His magnificent name, as the Psalms of David clearly do teach."[16]

"Trouble and fear are the very spurs to prayer; for when man, compassed about with vehement calamities, and vexed . . . does call to [Christ] for comfort and support from the deep pit of tribulation, such prayer ascends into [His presence], and returns not in vain."[17]

Knox on trusting Christ:

"Christ Jesus hath fought our battle. He Himself hath taken us into His care and protection. However the devil may rage by temptations, be they spiritual or corporeal, he is not able to bereave us out of the hand of the Almighty Son of God."[18]

"By the brightness of God's Scriptures we are brought to the feeling of God's wrath and anger, which by our manifold offences we have justly provoked against ourselves; which revelation and conviction God sends not of a purpose to confound us, but of very love, by which He had concluded our salvation to stand in Jesus Christ."[19]

"But the sons of God fight against sin; sob and mourn when they find themselves tempted to do evil; and if they fall, rise again with earnest and unfeigned repentance. They do these things, not by their power, but by the power of the Lord Jesus, apart from whom they can do nothing."[20]

Knox on his family:

"[I am experiencing] heaviness by reason of the late death of [my] dear bed-fellow [his wife Marjory]."[21]

"I never delight in the weeping of any of God's creatures; yea, I can scarcely well abide the tears of my own boys whom my own hand corrects."[22]

Knox on predestination:

"The doctrine of God's eternal predestination is so necessary to the church of God, that, without the same, can faith neither be truly taught, neither surely established; man can never be brought to true humility and knowledge of himself; neither yet can he be ravished in admiration of God's eternal goodness, and so moved to praise Him."[23]

"There is no way more proper to build and establish faith, than when we hear and undoubtedly do believe that our election ... consisteth not in ourselves, but in the eternal and immutable good pleasure of God ... Then only is our salvation in assurance, when we find the cause of the same in the bosom and counsel of God."[24]

Knox in The Scots Confession:

"For by nature we are so dead, blind, and perverse, that neither can we feel when we are pricked, see the light when it shines, nor assent to the will of God when it is revealed, unless the Spirit of the Lord Jesus quicken that which is dead, remove the darkness from our minds, and bow our stubborn hearts to the obedience of his blessed will."[25]

"The cause of good works, we confess, is not our free will, but the Spirit of the Lord Jesus, who dwells in our hearts by true faith."[26]

Knox writing to Calvin:

"I am prevented from writing to you more amply by a fever which afflicts me, by the weight of labors which oppress me, and the cannon of the French which they have now brought over to crush us . . . [Yet] He whose cause we defend will come to the aid of his own. Be mindful of us in your prayers."[27]

Recommended Knox Reading

To learn more about Knox's life, consider starting with the easy introductory biography *The Mighty Weakness of John Knox* by Douglas Bond. This work offers a quick but satisfactory glimpse at Knox's life that is honest about his faults but still tends to be overly positive, unlike most modern material that suffers heavily from the opposite fault. Another short biography worth consulting is *John Knox and the Reformation* written by the late great preacher Dr. M. Lloyd-Jones and the outstanding modern historian Iain H. Murray. In terms of a full-length treatment of Knox, nothing compares to Jane Dawson's magisterial *John Knox*. Not only is this biography full of top-notch scholarship, it is also an enjoyable and engaging read, though long. Dawson's work, unlike anything else currently available, manages to fairly treat Knox with both historical and contextual understanding, fair criticism, and appropriate praise. Dawson helps modern readers understand the complexity of a man who is often, and inaccurately, described as simply misogynist by revealing Knox's tender, loving, and respectful relationship with many female supporters as documented by heavy correspondence. For example, Dawson notes that, "many of [Knox's] most loyal and devoted spiritual kindred were women. His 'sisters', like Anne Locke, provided the spiritual comfort and material support that sustained him...these 'sisters' gave him an essential support group of friends."[28] Thankfully, there was more to Knox than his critics realized.

For those seeking to read Knox first hand, Knox's infamous *The First Blast of the Trumpet Against the Monstrous Regiment of Women* is not the ideal place to start, although it is essential reading for those who want the full picture (the same can be said for *A Faithful Admonition to the Professors of God's Truth in England*). Knox ignored wise council from Calvin in publishing this book and, in hindsight, so exaggerated his case and attacked his opponents that he created unnecessary challenges throughout the rest of his life.[29] That being said, Knox was responding to a moment in history when several violent (and anti-Reformation) female monarchs were brutally attacking the gospel cause throughout Europe. Instead, readers should start with a work that Knox jointly led, *The Scots Confession*, which can be read in one sitting. This work briefly and beautifully captures the heart of Knox's passion for the gospel. This work can be found in its entirety within Bond's biography. Another great place to start would be *The Select Practical Writings of John Knox* published by the Banner of Truth. Instead of trying to wade through the six volume *The Works of John Knox* (also published by the Banner of Truth) this is a more accessible, more focused, and more manageable look into Knox's personal life and writing. While Knox's *Book of Discipline* and *History of the Reformation in Scotland* are also worthwhile reads, his correspondence as highlighted in Dawson's biography provides a more intimate look into Knox's heart and mind.

"Without knowledge of self there is no knowledge of God...
Without knowledge of God there is no knowledge of self."

John Calvin
Institutes of the Christian Religion

GLORIOUS RUINS

Francis Schaeffer was known for describing humanity as "glorious ruins." In this, he was acknowledging the inherent glory, dignity, and value that each human has simply because they were created in the image of God, as Genesis 1 describes. Even so, Schaeffer's phrase also acknowledges, painfully, the effect of Genesis 3, how humanity fell into sin, how the world was broken, and how our glory was not removed but severely marred. Like the Coliseum, the ancient pyramids, or an English castle, every human being bears the marks both of their glorious design and the crumbling, destabilizing, and destructive effects of sin. While the most visibly broken of us might struggle to believe our glory, the most visibly successful of us might struggle to confess our ruin. Both realities are true, and yet, hope is found not in what we once were but rather what we are becoming in and through Christ: creatures restored, redeemed, and made new.

When studying Church history this is no less true. While the naysayers and critics shine flashlights upon the cracks and crevices of Luther, Calvin, and Knox, too many of the faithful blindfold themselves to these blemishes, imagining these men not as they were but rather as they are now in glory—sinless and perfect. Neither approach will do, for both are dishonest and ultimately unhelpful. One borders on slander and pride while the other embraces naivety and idolatry. When studying the likes of Luther, Calvin, and Knox, we must see them as we see ourselves, glorious ruins being made new.

Only with this framework can Church history serve us well. Were you shocked by the inconsistencies and sin of these men? Good. Take a look upon yourself, see where you likewise stumble and turn to Jesus in repentance and hope. Were you inspired by the bravery, zeal, and love of these men for God, his word, and his people? Good. Remember that the same Spirit dwells in you, Christian, and turn to Jesus in dependence and hope. Have you read this work as an unbeliever or seeker, not sure what you believe? Good. Consider whether this reality is not true of you. Are you not broken and cracked by your own heart and this world? And yet, are you not filled with a longing for meaning, a longing for glory, and a longing for goodness? The same God who made the world, who created every soul in history, including Luther, Calvin, and Knox, is the same God who created you. In this God's death and resurrection there is both a remedy for your ruin and a pathway for the glory God intended to shine out of you, as a reflection of his very own. Only in Christ is this found. And Christ can be found. Turn to his word, trust in his work, and celebrate this hope with his people.

The more we read Church history, the more we should see of ourselves and of Christ. Don't let pride keep you from seeing the ruin of others or yourself. But also, don't let it keep you from seeing the glory of his design and the assurance of his work in his people. Keep reading. Keep growing. Keep living in Christ until he calls you home to glory.

ABOUT THE AUTHOR

STEPHEN R. MOREFIELD (M.Div., Covenant Theological Seminary) pastors Christ Covenant Evangelical Presbyterian Church in the wonderful small town of Leoti, KS. Stephen and his wife, Morgan, have three children. He is the author of *Fierce Grace: 30 Days with King David*, the co-author of *Enduring Grace: 21 Days with the Apostle Peter*, and has written for *Gospel-Centered Discipleship*. Stephen currently chairs the Care of Candidates Committee of the Presbytery of the West (EPC). He is originally from Kansas City, holding tight to his love of the Chiefs, Royals, Jayhawks, Sporting, and, of course, good barbecue.

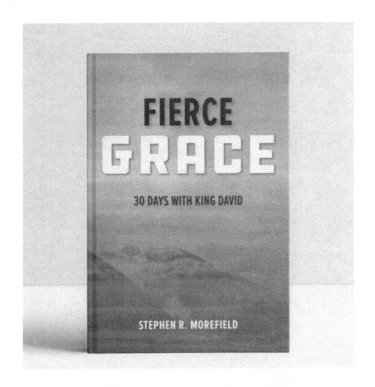

King David and his people lived broken, messy, and yet meaningful lives. In these thirty stories from 1 & 2 Samuel, Stephen Morefield explores the life of King David through the eyes of God's people. Both disappointment and hope will be found. And, while King David can't give us everything we need, he will point clearly to the One who can.

When tomorrow is harder than today, how will you endure? Peter preached boldly in one moment and cursed cowardly in another. His faith and obedience went up and down, down and up. But through it all, the grace of Jesus toward Peter endured. This is also how we will endure—through the amazing, enduring grace of God. In twenty-one stories, authors Stephen Morefield and Benjamin Vrbicek trace the life and teaching of the Apostle Peter as he followed Jesus. Peter's story gives us hope that Jesus really is a friend of sinners and mighty to save.

Introduction

[1] The Protestant Reformation or simply "The Reformation" is the phrase used to describe the efforts of many individuals and churches, within the Catholic Church, to correct major abuses including but not limited to the teaching of salvation by good works, the refusal to translate the Bible into the common languages, the supreme authority of the Pope, prayer to and worship of Mary and the Saints, the sale of indulgences for the forgiveness of sins, and many other Church traditions and customs that cannot be supported by the Bible. These actions reached a breaking (or official starting) point when the German monk Martin Luther publicly listed his objections in the form of his Ninety-Five Theses. Nearly all the Reformers first sought to fix the Catholic Church from within, hoping not to leave it, but were forced to eventually create new churches based on the teachings of the Bible that had been gradually lost within the Catholic Church over many centuries.

[2] Steven Lawson (quoting Philip Schaff), "The Reformation and the Men Behind it," *Ligonier Ministries,* October 1, 2018. Ligonier.org/blog/reformation-and-men-behind-it/.

Chapter 1

[1] R.C. Spoul and Stephen J. Nichols, eds, *The Legacy of Luther* (Chelsea, MI: Reformation Trust Publishing., 2016), 15–17.

[2] Ibid., 17.

[3] Steven J. Lawson, *The Heroic Boldness of Martin Luther* (Crawfordsville, IN: Reformation Trust Publishing, 2013), 5.

[4] Ibid., 5–6.

[5] Drew Blankman, *Martin Luther: Righteous Faith* (Downer's Grove, IL: InterVarsity Press, 2002), 14.

[6] "I regarded [Christ] only as a severe and terrible Judge." Lawson, *Boldness of Martin Luther,* 6.

[7] Resources utilized for this study of Romans 1 include F.F. Bruce, *Romans* (Downers Grove, IL: InterVarsity Press, 1985), R. Kent Hughes, *Romans* (Wheaton, IL: Crossway, 1991), Timothy Keller, *Romans 1–7 For You* (India: The Good Book Company, 2014), Martin Luther, *Commentary on Romans* (Grand Rapids, MI: Zondervan Publishing House, 1954), Douglas J. Moo, *The Letter To The Romans* (Grand Rapids, MI: William B. Eerdmans Publishing Company, 2018), and Thomas Schreiner, *Romans* (Grand Rapids, MI: Baker Academic, 1998). These resources were first used in composing a sermon on the topic and then those notes were used for this work. If anything deserving attribution was lost in the process, credit is due and sincerely given to these authors.

[8] Lawson, *Boldness of Martin Luther*, 12.

[9] Ibid., 9.

[10] Sproul, *Legacy of Luther*, 28.

[11] Martin Luther, *Romans*, 40–41.

[12] See also Philippians 3:9, 2 Corinthians 5:21, and Romans 5:17.

[13] Schreiner, *Romans,* 63.

[14] Keller, *Romans*, 21.

[15] Romans 3:23

[16] Romans 1:18

[17] Schreiner, *Romans,* 62.

[18] Keller, *Romans 1–7*, 20.

[19] Schreiner, *Romans,* 61.

[20] Moo, *Romans,* 70; "Faith is not (primarily) agreement with a set of doctrines but trust in a person."

[21] Sproul, *Legacy of Luther*, 7–8.

[22] For example, Ephesians 2:1–10, Colossians 2:13, and Romans 6:23.

[23] Sproul, *Legacy of Luther*, 1, 66–67. William Boekestein's short and helpful biography on Zwingli, entitled *Ulrich Zwingli*, helpfully explains the relationship from Zwingli's perspective.

[24] Lawson, *Boldness of Martin Luther*, 18.

[25] Sproul, *Legacy of Luther*, 39–40.

Chapter 2

[1] Sproul, *Legacy of Luther*, 3.

[2] Martin Luther, *The Bondage of the Will* (Grand Rapids, MI: Baker Publishing Group, 1957), 62.

[3] Sproul, *Legacy of Luther*, 2.

[4] Luther, *Bondage*, 71.

[5] Ibid., 68–70, 91.

[6] Lawson, *Boldness of Martin Luther*, 49.

[7] Ibid., 106–107.

[8] Luther, *Bondage,* 73–74.

⁹ Ibid., 63, 74, 88.

¹⁰ Lawson, *Boldness of Martin Luther*, 14–15.

¹¹ Luther, *Bondage*, 87.

¹² These quotes come, with appropriate sourcing, from the fantastic and hilarious website known as the "Lutheran Insulter." Check it out here: ergofabulous.org/luther.

¹³ Lawson, *Boldness of Martin Luther*, 19.

¹⁴ Sproul, *Legacy of Luther*, 75–93.

¹⁵ Ibid., 14.

¹⁶ Lawson, *Boldness of Martin Luther*, 97.

¹⁷ Sproul, *Legacy of Luther*, 263–264.

¹⁸ Lawson, *Boldness of Martin Luther*, 10–11.

¹⁹ Luther, *Bondage*, 78–79.

²⁰ Ibid., 83–84, 104.

²¹ Jim West, *Drinking with Calvin and Luther!* (Lincoln, CA: Oakdown, 2003), 29.

²² Ibid., 34–35.

²³ Luther, *Romans* , 40–41.

²⁴ Sproul, *Legacy of Luther*, 3–4.

²⁵ Luther's harsh comments towards the Jewish people are inexcusable but not unforgivable if we believe in the same gospel that Luther did. Indeed, Luther struggled throughout his life with anger spilled out harshly through his words, both written and spoken. While Luther's words clearly reveal racism, his attitude toward the Jewish people in later years is inconsistent with the love he felt for the Old Testament people of God, his tireless work to translate the Old Testament, and his genuine ministry efforts toward his Jewish neighbors. In the end, this is certainly a case of serious sin, frustration at the largely negative response his Jewish

neighbors had toward the gospel, and his belief that these neighbors were seeking to covert people away from Christianity. Sadly, while this sin does not nullify Luther's legacy, it has stained his ministry and, unknown to Luther, was later used by the Nazi regime to justify genocide. While we often rejoice in Luther's colorful and creative language, the danger that James warns of concerning sinful language is ever on display in this sad chapter of Luther's life. See Sproul, *Legacy of Luther,* 66–67.

Chapter 3

[1] T.H.L Parker, *Portrait of Calvin* (Minneapolis, MN: Desiring God, 2001), 35–36.

[2] Bruce Gordon, *Calvin* (New Haven, CT: Yale University Press, 2009), 64–65.

[3] Resources utilized for this study of Ephesians 4:11–16 included John Calvin, *Commentaries on the Epistles of Paul to the Galatians and Ephesians* (Grand Rapids, MI: Baker Books, 2009), Bryan Chapell, *Ephesians* (Phillipsburg, NJ: P&R Publishing, 2009), and Francis Foulkes, *Ephesians* (Downers Grove, IL: InterVarsity Press, 1989). These resources were first used in composing a sermon on the topic and then those notes were used for this work. If anything deserving attribution was lost in the process, credit is due and sincerely given to these authors.

[4] Ephesians 2:11–22 and 4:4–6.

[5] Ephesians 4:7, 11–16.

[6] Chapell, *Ephesians*, 187.

[7] Foulkes, *Ephesians*, 123–126.

[8] For a lengthier discussion of this point see: Jeramie Rinne, *Church Elders* (Wheaton, IL; Crossway, 2014).

[9] Calvin, *Ephesians*, 285; Foulkes, *Ephesians,* 129.

[10] Lawson, *Boldness of Martin* Luther, 26–28; Sproul, *The Legacy of Luther*, 107, Alister McGrath, "The State of the Church

Before the Reformation," *White Horse Inn,* March 1, 1995, https://www.whitehorseinn.org/article/the-state-of-the-church-before-the-reformation/.

[11] Gordon, *Calvin*, 138, 288, 300, John Starke, "John Calvin, Missionary and Church Planter" *The Gospel Coalition*, November 27, 2012, https://www.thegospelcoalition.org/article/john-calvin-missionary-and-church-planter/

[12] Chapell, *Ephesians*, 190.

[13] John Piper, "Is Every Christian a Saint?" *Desiring God*, June 22, 2017, https://www.desiringgod.org/labs/is-every-christian-a-saint.

[14] Foulkes, *Ephesians,* 127.

[15] Foulkes puts this well: "Christians are to hold forth the truth in order to bring spiritual benefits to others, and they are to do so with a winsomeness that only love can make possible." Foulkes, *Ephesians*, 129. See also Chapell, *Ephesians*, 199.

[16] Calvin, *Ephesians.*

[17] Gordon, *Calvin,* 128, 200–202.

[18] See Chapell's discussion of this topic in Chapell, *Ephesians*, 194–198.

[19] 1 Corinthians 5 & 11.

[20] Parker, *Portrait*, 42–44.

[21] Ibid., 74.

[22] Ibid., 74–75.

[23] Ibid., 42.

[24] Gordon, *Calvin*, 144–145, 278–279.

[25] Ibid., vii, 91, 144–145.

[26] John Calvin, *A Little Book on the Christian Life* (Ann Arbor, MI: Reformation Trust Publishing, 2017), 14–16.

Chapter 4

1 Parker, *Portrait of Calvin*, 32.

2 Gordon, *Calvin*, 148.

3 Ibid., 147.

4 John Calvin, A Little Book on the Christian Life, IV.

5 Gordon, *Calvin,* 112.

6 Parker, *Portrait*, 12.

7 Calvin, *Christian Life*, 104.

8 Parker, *Portrait*, 70–71.

9 Ibid., 71.

10 Ibid., *Portrait,* 33.

11 Calvin, *Christian Life*, 108.

12 Parker, *Portrait*, 80.

13 Calvin, *Ephesians*, 278.

14 Ibid., 278–82.

15 Ibid., 288.

16 Parker, *Portrait*, 83.

17 Ibid., 30.

18 West, *Drinking*, 53.

19 Ibid., 58.

20 Parker, *Portrait*, 63.

21 Gordon, *Calvin*, 131.

22 Calvin, *Christian Life*, 13.

23 Ibid., 73–74.

24 Gordon, *Calvin,* 334.

25 Gordon, *Calvin*, 3.

26 Douglas Bond, *The Mighty Weakness of John Knox* (Crawfordsville, IN: Reformation Trust Publishing, 2011), 81.

27 While Calvin was a far from perfect man, the execution of Servetus in Geneva is hardly the crushing flaw of Calvin's life as it is often made out to be. Gordon fairly discusses Servetus's ongoing behavior and the lack of power Calvin actually had in the final result. Calvin indeed pleaded for Servetus to be spared. Gordon, *Calvin*, 43, 195, 212, 217–233, 235, 240, 269–270, 280, 301.

Chapter 5

1 Jane Dawson, *John Knox* (New Haven, CT: Yale University Press, 2015), 54–56; See also Bond, *Knox*, 9–11.

2 Ibid.

3 Resources utilized for this study of John 17 included D. A. Carson, *The Gospel According to John* (Grand Rapids, MI: William B. Eerdmans Publishing Company, 1991), Colin G. Kruse, *John* (Downers Grove, IL: InterVarsity Press, 2003), Richard D. Phillips, *John* (Philipsburg, NJ: P&R Publishing, 2014), and *Robert* W. Yarbrough, *John* (Chicago: Moody Press, 1991). These resources were first used in composing a sermon on the topic and then those notes were used for this work. If anything deserving attribution was lost in the process, credit is due and sincerely given to these authors

4 Dawson, *John Knox*, 26–30.

5 Yarbrough, *John*, 175; Kruse, *John*, 340.

6 Yarbrough, *John*, 171.

7 "What belongs to the Father, however, belongs no less to the Son." Carson, *John*, 561. See also Yarbrough, *John*, 173; Kruse, *John*, 336.

8 "This gift was not rooted in anything intrinsic to the people themselves." Carson, *John*, 558, see also 555.

[9] Dawson, *John Knox,* 11.

[10] Ibid., 14–15.

[11] Ibid., 17–19.

[12] Ibid., 20.

[13] Bond, *Knox,* 3–5.

[14] Ibid., 86.

[15] Yarbrough, *John,* 174.

[16] Kruse, *John*, 338.

[17] Ibid., 339.

[18] Carson, *John,* 566–567.

[19] Yarbrough, *John, 175.*

[20] Bond, *Knox,* 6–11.

[21] Dawson, *John Knox*, 58–59.

[22] Dawson, *John Knox,* 286–287; Bond, *Knox,* 26.

[23] Bond, *Knox,* 19–22.

[24] Carson, *John*, 570.

[25] Bond, *Knox*, 91.

[26] Jane Dawson fairly and consistently deals with these flaws and more in her biography. See especially the book's conclusion. See also, Bond, *Knox*, 17.

[27] Dawson, *John Knox*, 310.

[28] Ibid., 27.

[29] A. Taylor Innes, *John Knox* (Edinburgh: Oliphant Anderson and Ferrier; 1896), 29.

Chapter 6

[1] Dawson, *John Knox*, 9, 20.

2 Bond, *Knox,* 69.

3 Ibid., 69, 73.

4 Ibid., 73.

5 Dawson, *John Knox,* 69–70, 232–233, 319.

6 Bond, *Knox*, 1.

7 Parish, Helen and William G. Naphy, eds, *Religion and Superstition in Reformation Europe* (New York: Manchester University Press, 2002) 135.

8 Lawson, Steven J. *Famine in the Land: A Passionate Call for Expository Preaching* (Chicago; Moody Publishers, 2003), 94.

9 Bond, *Knox*, 51.

10 Ibid., 63.

11 Ibid., 26.

12 Ibid., 57.

13 Ibid., 14.

14 Ibid., 15.

15 Ibid., 22.

16 Cochrane, Robert, ed, *The Treasury of British Eloquence* (London: William P. Nimmo, 1878), 18.

17 Bond, *Knox,* 42.

18 Ibid., 29.

19 Ibid., 32.

20 Ibid., 60.

21 Ibid., 90–92.

22 Ibid., 92.

23 Ibid., 79, 85.

[24] Ibid., 86.

[25] Ibid., 119.

[26] Ibid., 120

[27] Ibid., 31.

[28] Dawson, *John Knox,* 69–70, 232–233, 319.

[29] Bond, *Knox,* 17–19.